WHAT BUSINESS LEADERS ARE SAYING ABOUT
A Life of Excellence

"Richard Simmons's presentation on charting a path that can enable us to meet our personal goals and accomplish the things that are important to us was magnificent. He has a true gift for making a complicated topic easy to understand."

—Billy Bates, Managing Partner, Starnes Davis Florie

"Richard Simmons addresses one of the most important issues we face: how do we bridge the gap between our dreams for our lives and the reality of the lives we actually lead?"

— Norman Jetmundsen, VP and Associate General Counsel
Vulcan Materials Company

"Richard's message directly correlated with the bank's core values and will make us a better company."

—Forest Whatley, Managing Director, Oakworth Capital Bank

"If you or your organization are looking for someone to deliver a positive message that can help each individual, I highly encourage you to consider Richard Simmons. I am confident that our staff will reap future benefits by putting his suggestions into action."

—Grantland Rice III, President, Cobbs Allen

A LIFE *of* EXCELLENCE

Wisdom for Effective Living

Richard E. Simmons III

UNION HILL
PUBLISHING

A Life of Excellence

Wisdom for Effective Living

Copyright © 2013 Richard E. Simmons III

Union Hill is the book publishing imprint of
The Center for Executive Leadership,
a 501(c)3 nonprofit organization.
www.TheCenterBham.org

Casebound ISBN 978-1-939358-01-1
Paperback ISBN 978-1-939358-11-0
eBook ISBN 978-1-939358-04-2

Printed in the United States of America

4 5 6 7 8 9 0

The quality of a man's life is in direct proportion to his commitment to excellence.
—Vince Lombardi, Hall of Fame NFL Coach

Contents

A LIFE *of* EXCELLENCE

Preface

I remember reading about excellence a number of years ago in the writings of Dr. Dallas Willard, a brilliant philosophy professor and former director of the philosophy department at the University of Southern California. Willard wrote about excellence in the lives of great athletes who had reached their full potential. He concluded that without exception each of these athletes had chosen an overall life of preparation of mind and body, investing a great deal of time and energy into a rigorous daily regimen that few others would ever see. In all likelihood, behind each great accomplishment one would also discover failure, heartbreak, defeats, and setbacks.

We make a fundamental mistake when we just marvel at glamorous end results. Finally, Willard writes: "What is true of specific activities is, of course, also true of life as a whole. As Plato long ago saw, there is an art to living, and the living is excellent only when the self is prepared in all the depths and dimensions of its being."

Deep down, we all know that a life of excellence is possible, yet we so often lack the will to follow through on what we know to be true. It is important to point out that when I use the word "excellence" it means being the best you can be. It's not about trying to be better than everyone else in your sphere of influence. Too often we measure our achievements and ourselves by how we compare with others. We often find ourselves asking: "What do people think of me? How do they rate me, my family, and my accomplishments?"

Without realizing it, we end up gearing our lives to meet the expectations of others. Such behavior is not only an unhealthy way to live our lives but can also create all kinds of problems for us. Legendary basketball coach John Wooden said that one of the most important teachings he received from his father was: "Don't worry about being better than somebody else, but never cease trying to be the best you can be. You have control over that, not the other."

Wooden said he never forgot those words because he realized that his father was trying to teach him to judge his success in basketball, school, and ultimately life based on how hard he worked to fulfill his own God-given potential. I encourage you to seek to be your very best, to seek a life of excellence, but to be content with who you are, what you have, and what you have been able to accomplish. God doesn't care how you compare with your neighbor. He cares for how well you employ your time, your talent, and the resources He has given you.

* * *

In my work, I've observed how modern people seem to drift through life with little or no sense of real direction. Their lives are buffeted by nothing more than their reactions to the circumstances they face each day. They have trouble finding that path which leads to serious learning and growth and the development of new skills. They seem to have no idea how to make life conform to their hopes and dreams. As the years go by, I see more and more of these people facing the stark realization that they haven't reached their God-given potential. And they know that time is running out.

This is a short and simple book about how to live more effectively and wisely in the most important areas of your life. It focuses on how to live more "intentionally" by looking at three simple but crucial principles. If you leverage these principles to your advantage, they will enable you to live a much more productive and contented life. Ultimately, this book seeks to answer the question that frustrates most people: "Why is there such a gap between the life I have aspired to and the life I am actually living now?"

My hope is to help you dramatically shrink that gap.

Introduction

Almost twenty-five years ago, my life was deeply impacted
by a scene in a movie. Tom Schulman's screenplay of the
classic film *Dead Poets Society* had a powerful opening,
which I have never forgotten. It's the first day of class at
Welton Academy, a very fine prep school for young men.
Welton is steeped in history and tradition. Mr. Keating,
a new English teacher (played by Robin Williams), calls
the class to order. He then surprises them by marching
the class out into the hall to look at some old black-and-
white photos enclosed in trophy cases lining the walls.
These photos are of young men who attended Welton
more than half a century earlier. "We are food for worms,
lads," he tells his class, as they look at the photos.

> *Believe it or not, each and every one of us in this room
> is one day going to stop breathing, turn cold, and die. I
> would like you to peruse some of the faces from the past.
> You've walked by them many times, but I don't think
> you've really looked at them.*

They're not that different from you, are they? Same haircuts. Full of hormones, just like you. Invincible, just like you feel. The world is their oyster. They believe they are destined for great things, just like many of you. Their eyes are full of hope, just like you. Did they wait until it was too late to make from their lives even one iota of what they were capable? Because you see, gentlemen, these boys are now fertilizing daffodils. If you listen real close you can hear them whisper their legacy to you. Go on, lean in. Do you hear it?

As the boys curiously lean in toward the glass enclosure, Professor Keating whispers in their ears, "Car-pe, car-pe, carpe diem. Seize the day, boys! Make your lives extraordinary!" Then he leaves them with these powerful words: "Since your destiny is yet to be determined, why not make it extraordinary and leave a lasting legacy?"

Mr. Keating recognizes one of the great flaws in human beings—we are, by our very nature, short-term in our thinking, so he presents these young men with a very powerful challenge. What do you want your life to have been about when you get to the end of it? Like most of us, these young men don't immediately get the point—that taking a longer-term perspective will lead to better decisions in the present. This is also the central challenge in this book, presented in the form of three questions:

- How can I make a lasting difference?
- What path must I take in order to reach my full potential?
- How do I want to be remembered when my life is over?

In stepping back to give serious consideration to these questions, each of us has an opportunity to discover the path that can dramatically alter the course and trajectory of our lives.

Chapter 1
The Pain of Regret

*No individual has any right to come into the world and
go out of it without leaving behind him distinct
and legitimate reasons for having passed through it.*
—George Washington Carver

President Jimmy Carter has shared a *powerful* encounter
he experienced as a young naval officer; an event that he
says shaped his life. In order to be considered for an officer's position on a nuclear submarine, the candidate first
had to be interviewed and approved by Admiral Hyman
Rickover, who at the time was head of the United States
Nuclear Navy. Here is how President Carter described
the interview:

*I had applied for the nuclear submarine program, and
Admiral Rickover was interviewing me for the job. It
was the first time I met Admiral Rickover, and we sat
in a large room by ourselves for more than two hours,*

and he let me choose any subjects I wished to discuss. Very carefully, I chose those about which I knew most at the time — current events, seamanship, music, literature, naval tactics, electronics, gunnery — and he began to ask me a series of questions of increasing difficulty. In each instance, he soon proved that I knew relatively little about the subject I had chosen. He always looked right into my eyes, and he never smiled. I was saturated with cold sweat. Finally, he asked a question and I thought I could redeem myself. He said, "How did you stand in your class at the Naval Academy?" Since I had completed my sophomore year at Georgia Tech before Annapolis as a plebe, I had done very well, and I swelled my chest with pride and answered, "Sir, I stood fifty-ninth in a class of 820!" I sat back to wait for the congratulations — which never came. Instead, the question, "Did you do your best?"

I started to say, "Yes, sir," but I remembered who this was and recalled several of the many times at the Academy when I could have learned more about our allies, our enemies, weapons, strategy, and so forth. I was just human. I finally gulped and said, "No, sir, I didn't always do my best."

He looked at me for a long time, and then turned his

chair around to end the interview. He asked one final question, which I have never been able to forget — or to answer. He said, "Why not?"

I sat there for a while, shaken, and slowly left the room.

This encounter caused Carter to completely alter the direction of his life, and later inspired his best-selling book *Why Not the Best?* Admiral Rickover's powerful words to Carter have made me wonder if I have even come close to doing my best in this life, and whether, in reality, anyone ever really does his or her very best? Rickover's final question to Carter seems very pointed and appropriate: "If you have not done your best... why not?"

Another Perspective

Best-selling author and noted business consultant Stephen Covey takes a slightly different approach to confronting this same issue. He poses a series of questions:

What is the one activity that you know if you did superbly well and consistently would have significant results in your personal life? And what is the one activity that you know if you did superbly well and consistently would have significant positive results in your professional or work life? And if you know these things would make such a significant difference, why are you not doing them right now?

Covey concludes there is one primary reason we seldom pursue these activities: We do not consider them with any real sense of urgency. We most likely recognize that they are important but just not pressing. Therefore we procrastinate, with the justification "I will get to it later."

I am not sure we fully understand that the important activities of life so often don't act on us; we must make clear and conscious choices to act on them. This lack of understanding is perhaps why so many of us spend our lives reacting to the urgent demands of life and then wonder why we're unable to focus on the important activities that will make a significant and lasting difference. As a result, in our day-to-day decision making, the "urgent" seems to dominate over the "important," and thus we end up with very little personal growth and, at best, a mediocre life.

I believe Covey is right. We have this tendency to drift through life without pursuing meaningful objectives. Research indicates that most people in Western societies do not have a clearly defined strategy or mission for their lives. They live reactively. Their lives become nothing more than a response to the circumstances that are presented to them each day, increasingly in the form of tweets, posts, and emails. Modern people seem to be bound to a frenetic lifestyle, merely doing what is most urgent and immediate.

This reflects what Pulitzer Prize-winning novelist John Cheever said many years ago: "The main emotion of the adult American, who has all the advantages of wealth, education, and culture, is disappointment."

Too many adults, particularly as they near the end of their lives, experience the awful pain of regret as they reflect on a life that could have been.

Several years ago, Bob and Judy Fisher, a husband-and-wife team living in Nashville, Tennessee, wrote an interesting book on the subject of long-term thinking. Their book, entitled *Life is a Gift*, focuses on, among other things, a life of regret. The Fishers interviewed 104 terminally ill patients, all of them under hospice care. In each case there was a recurring theme:

So many people realized too late that there was a significant gap between the things they ought to be doing in their lives, and the things they actually did.

Now contrast this with the life of author C. S. Lewis. If you have ever read about Lewis' personal life, you will have discovered that he led a very well ordered and disciplined life. He maintained great relationships and truly lived an exceptional life. Lewis passed away at age sixty-five, yet a week before he died, he said to his brother Warren: "I have done all that I was sent into the world to do, I am ready to go."

What a stark contrast with the hospice patients the Fishers interviewed, who so painfully revealed the regrets in their lives. Aren't the words of C. S. Lewis what we would all like to be able to say at the end of our lives?

I believe that we're all capable of doing just that, but it all depends on what we are doing right now.

Chapter 2
"Good Enough" Never Is

*The lesson of history is that, to the degree people
and civilizations have operated in harmony with
correct principles, they have prospered.*
— Steven Covey

It was almost fifty years ago, yet former quarterback Bart
Starr still vividly recalls his first encounter with the man
who would change his life. The new head coach of the
Green Bay Packers, Vince Lombardi, was introduced to
the team, which had won only one of their twelve games
the previous season. This is how Starr remembered that
first meeting:

*He opened the session by thanking the Packers
for allowing him to be their coach. This tells you
something about the man. Then he quickly turned to
us and said, "Gentlemen, we are going to relentlessly
chase perfection, knowing full well we will not catch*

7

it, because nothing is perfect. But we are going to relentlessly chase it, because in the process we will catch excellence." He came right up on us, within a foot of us in the front row, and then he said, "I am not remotely interested in just being good."

In his nine years with the Packers, Lombardi led the team to five NFL championships and memorable victories in the first two Super Bowls.

I think we all would agree that the notion of achieving a life of excellence has great appeal and even sounds rather noble. But what is this life of excellence and what exactly might it look like?

The word "excellence" comes from two Latin root words that together mean: "to rise out from." Excellence, then, is the quality of rising to one's expected potential. Specifically, we're referring to the unique potential and abilities that God has endowed us with. At its core, the responsibility of developing one's talents becomes a stewardship issue. A person can choose to be extraordinarily productive or choose to squander the gifts uniquely bestowed by God.

Dr. Tom Morris, a former philosophy professor at Notre Dame, says that excellence "is to be the best you can be in everything you do, across a broad range of activities, compatible with the realities of your situation."

This idea of personal excellence is not something new. Socrates addressed the issue over 2,400 years ago. He said that we have been deceived into thinking that success and wealth will bring personal excellence into our lives. However, in reality, personal excellence will bring true success and true wealth into our lives, affording both the public and private blessings in life.

* * *

I recently had an opportunity to spend some time with Dr. Kevin Elko. Over the past few years Elko has been working with Coach Nick Saban on developing the psychological and motivational skills of the University of Alabama football team. I asked Dr. Elko about Coach Saban's views on the development of his players, and I learned that Saban stresses the players' individual focus on the process, not the wins and losses or even national championships.

Elko explained that this process involves Coach Saban getting his team to develop a single-minded focus on "striving for excellence" in all areas of their lives, both on and off the field. This includes excellence in the weight room and excellence in learning the fundamentals of the game, as well as learning the complicated schemes the team employs. It involves excellence in off-season programs. It demands individual moral excellence, academic excellence, and finally, with Dr. Elko's assistance, a sharp focus on the emotional and psychological well-being of each player. Coach Saban is convinced that if his players will concentrate on the process, the wins and losses will take care of themselves.

Based on the team's actual performance, this strategy has worked quite well.

The Place to Start

The best place to begin this pursuit of excellence is to understand how life is designed. God designed life so that there is a pattern or fabric to all of reality. Consequently, life is governed by certain laws and principles. These are not "good" or" bad," "moral" or "immoral." they are simply true. However, what is crucial for us to grasp is that these principles actually make life predictable. Such an understanding creates the potential for more predictable outcomes in our lives. Most significantly, our lives will flourish when they are in harmony with these principles.

Stephen Covey writes:

Principles always have natural consequences attached to them. There are positive consequences when we live in harmony with the principles. There are negative consequences when we ignore them. But because these principles apply to everyone, whether or not they are aware, this limitation is universal. And the more we know of correct principles, the greater is our ability to live wisely. By centering our lives on timeless, unchanging principles, we create a fundamental paradigm of effective living.

Covey is clear that you cannot violate these fundamental principles with impunity. Whether we believe in them or not, these unchanging principles have proven to be valid throughout all of human history.

As you continue to read, I will lay out three principles that will clearly point you toward a life of excellence. I hope you will see that if you live in accordance with these principles, your life will flourish.

The Choices We Make

This first principle is, I believe, the most important one in all of life as regards effective living. In fact, as simple as it is, I believe this principle will ultimately determine the outcome of your life.

It begins with what is known as the wisdom literature of the Bible (Psalms and Proverbs). There is a word that is used consistently throughout these two books, and its literal meaning is the foundation of this first principle.

The word I refer to is "way." You can see how it's used in the following verses.

- Proverbs 4:11 – I have directed you in the way of wisdom.

- Proverbs 9:6 – Proceed in the way of understanding.

- Psalm 119:104 – I hate every false way.

- Proverbs 16:25 – There is a way that seems right to a man, but its end is the way of death.

In each of these verses, you see the word "way" used in the teaching. It is derived from the Hebrew word *derek,* which means "road" or "pathway. We are being told that each of us is on a pathway that is leading us in a certain direction.

That last verse, Proverbs 16:25, makes it clear that there is a pathway that appears to be good and right but in fact leads us in a direction that will bring pain, regret, and possibly destruction into our lives. While it may seem like the right path at the outset, it is not. Eventually it leads to dead ends. On the other hand, there are paths that lead to our well-being, and there is a path that leads to individual excellence.

Several years ago, I read Andy Stanley's wonderful book *The Principle of the Path*. In it, Stanley explains why so many of us never reach our full potential. This principle he writes about, while simple, is quite profound, and is of critical importance if you want to live an exceptional life — a life of excellence.

The Principle of the Path is simply this: We are all on a path right now, whether we realize it or not. And this path is taking each of us to a certain destination. The path we are on is not a respecter of persons; it does not care who you are or where you are from. It leads where it leads regardless of one's talent, wealth, physical appearance, or social status.

The best way to visualize this principle is to consider this question: When you meet someone who has achieved excellence and is leading a truly extraordinary life in all areas, how do you think this person's life has come to pass? Do you believe it was an accident or a stroke of good fortune? What we always discover is that people are where they are in life as a result of a series of decisions that together have formed the path leading to their present circumstances.

I had a man share with me that his son attended a football camp at the University of Alabama in the summer of 2010. The previous football season, Mark Ingram had won the Heisman Trophy as a sophomore. During the camp, a few of the boys were on the field at 7:00 AM going through some drills. On the other side of the field was Mark Ingram, with a graduate assistant, working on his receiving skills.

Mark Ingram did not win the Heisman trophy and become an NFL first-round draft choice because he was lucky or because of his talent. He got on a path that enabled him to develop his skills so that he could become an exceptional football player.

On the other hand, when you see people floundering in their personal lives, quite often their stories reveal a pattern or path as well. It's amazing how we can deceive ourselves into thinking that life is simply a series of unrelated decisions and that somehow we will just end up with lives of excellence.

The Principle of the Path is at work in your life every minute of every day. Right now, for example, you are on a physical health path and it is taking you in a specific direction. In all likelihood, this path will impact the length of your life and the quality of your life in old age.

Likewise, your marriage is on a certain path at this very moment. It will determine the kind of life you will experience with your spouse as the years go by. If you have children at home, you are on a child-rearing path, and that path will determine the types of people your children will become. We are each on a financial path, a moral path, an intellectual path, a career path, and a spiritual path. The paths we are on always determine our end results. Always!

Chapter 3
Understanding Ourselves

*What great accomplishments we would have
in the world if everybody had done what they
had intended to do.*
—Frank Clark

I think most people will tell you they believe the Principle of the Path is true. The problem is, though they may say they believe it, they don't live their lives as if it were true. This chapter presents three reasons why there's such a startling gap between what we desire in our hearts and what we end up doing with our lives. As you read these words, my hope is you will come to an even better understanding of yourself. Perhaps you will uncover some hidden personal flaws that keep you from making wise choices.

What I find so baffling is that most people are inclined to choose paths that do not lead them in the direction of their intended hopes and dreams. The question is why?

Why are there such discrepancies between what we actually desire in our hearts and what we end up doing with our lives? For example, no one begins his journey with the desire to end up frittering away his talents and abilities, but regrettably, this is what so often happens. Why is this? Why do people not do their best? Why do we not strive for and achieve personal excellence?

There are three primary reasons.

Good Intentions

The first and most crucial point to understand is that in the midst of decision making, most people lean hard on their intentions and dreams but pay little attention to the actual paths they have chosen. Good intentions will not get you where you want to go. At the end of the day, it's the direction of the path, not one's intentions, that ultimately determine a person's destination.

I founded The Center for Executive Leadership when I began to notice a pattern in the lives of so many men. Once they had graduated from college, business school, or law school, most seemed to know what they wanted for their lives. They all anticipated rewarding careers and hoped to earn a great deal of money over their lifetimes. Each desired to marry a beautiful woman and enjoy a fulfilling marriage. All wanted to have perfect children and live the American Dream. Now fast-forward fifteen or twenty years and it began to dawn on them: their lives had not turned out the way they had imagined. The American Dream had not happened for them. While it's natural to want to have a good career, a wonderful marriage, and healthy children who flourish, the problem for so many is that the dream never becomes a reality. Very few people ask themselves at the outset of their journey "What is the path that will take me to this destination?"

In the July 2010 *Harvard Business Review* there is an article written by Clayton Christiansen, a Rhodes Scholar who attended Harvard Business School and who currently teaches there. Christiansen writes:

Over the years I have watched the fates of my Harvard Business School classmates from 1979 unfold. I have seen more and more of them come to reunions unhappy, divorced, and alienated from their children. I can guarantee that not a single one of them graduated with the deliberate strategy of getting divorced and raising children who would be estranged from them.

Yet they went down a path that led to this consequence. How could this possibly have happened?

I recently visited with a father whose son attended a large state university here in the South. He shared that during his son's four years of college, six of the young men in his fraternity had died of either drug overdose or alcohol asphyxiation.

I thought of these promising young men as college freshmen. Each, I am sure, had great hopes and dreams for the future. I imagine that none of them had any intention of seeing his life unexpectedly cut short. Each of them, however, chose a path that would eventually lead to his tragic and premature death.

No one has a deliberate strategy to begin his adult life only to end up with a wasted life, but this is what so often happens. We all have good intentions, but at the end of the day, it is the direction of the path, not good intentions, that will ultimately determine our destination in life.

Truth and Wisdom

A second reason we do not achieve excellence in our personal lives is because so many people are not on a quest for truth and wisdom but rather on a search for pleasure and happiness. We are often guided by our feelings and emotions instead of by wise judgment. In other words, our quest for pleasure and happiness in the now takes priority over sound decision making that will positively impact our lives in the future.

As one keen observer has noted, people of this world are like children in their approach to life. If you were to offer a child a piece of cake or a $10,000 Treasury bond, he will almost always choose the cake. Children invariably choose immediate gratification without giving consideration to future consequences. They do not understand the value and significance of delayed gratification, yet so many adults today seem to be no different. They almost always choose temporary feel-good pleasures over that which has lasting value.

I have concluded that most people today do not fully understand the complexity of the human heart and its desires. Have you ever noticed how contradictory your desires can be? For instance, a young man may choose to stay out late partying with his friends, but at the same time he wants to excel in his career by getting to work early. Notice there is an obvious conflict in this young man's desires.

Our wants, while endless, are often not in harmony with each other. Modern people seem to gravitate toward those desires that bring pleasure and happiness—like the young man who wants to stay out late with his friends but also wants to excel in his job. Wisdom, however, recognizes the importance of discovering which desires are liberating and which are destructive. Which of my desires are in harmony with who I really am and with what I really desire to do with my life?

One of the most gifted writers ever to live was the English author and poet Oscar Wilde. He was educated in some of Great Britain's finest schools and excelled in the Greek language. His writing earned him great wealth and he was the toast of London. One literary critic described him as "our most quotable writer" after Shakespeare. Sadly, however, Wilde squandered all that he had and died penniless. Before he died, he reflected on his life and penned these words:

I must say to myself that I ruined myself, and that nobody great or small can be ruined except by his own hand.... Terrible as what the world did to me, what I did to myself was far more terrible still. The gods had given me almost everything. But I let myself be lured into long spells of senseless and sensual ease. I surrounded myself with the smaller natures and the meaner minds. I became the spendthrift of my own genius, and to waste an eternal youth gave me a curious joy. Tired of being on the heights, I deliberately went to the depths in search for new sensation. What the paradox was to me in the sphere of thought, perversity became to me in the sphere of passion. Desire, at the end, was a malady, or a madness, or both.

I grew careless of the lives of others. I took pleasure where it pleased me, and passed on. I forgot that every little action of the common day makes or unmakes character, and that therefore what one has done in the secret chamber one has some day to cry aloud on the housetop. I ceased to be lord over myself. I was no longer the captain of my soul, and did not know it.

Wilde desired to live a long life and produce great literary work, but he also loved pleasure. In the end, as he put it himself, "I allowed pleasure to dominate me. I ended in horrible disgrace."

Wilde died a broken man at the age of forty-six.

* * *

One of our family's mottoes comes from the book *Do Hard Things.* As I tell my children, the path that leads to excellence is in fact often the most difficult, but if we persist in our efforts while going down difficult paths, over time they will become easier. This is not because the nature of the task has changed but because our ability to do it has grown.

My wife provides a good example of this. Though she exercises regularly, she decided a little over a year ago as a personal challenge to take up swimming. The problem is that she did not grow up swimming. The first time she swam laps in the pool, she swallowed a good bit of water. There was nothing enjoyable about the experience; however, she persisted, and over time her swimming improved and the difficult workouts became easier. She has now reached the point where she no longer dreads the pool but sees and feels the benefits that come from swimming.

Writer John Piper was correct when he said, "All training is painful and frustrating as you seek to develop certain skills. However, over time, as these skills become second nature, they lead to greater joy."

It is crucial to understand that if we invest time each day in important activities and skill development, we will eventually become very capable. Repetition is the key to enhancing our skills. This is how we build certain habits and disciplines into our lives. The question we should consider is this: Am I now on a truth and wisdom quest? Is my life in harmony with what is true, regardless of how difficult that truth may be?

The significance of this resonated with me over twenty years ago when I read a quote from Jack Welch. Welch is famous for having taken General Electric, a dying dinosaur of a company, and transforming it into one of the world's greatest corporations. A guiding principle in Welch's approach to running G.E. was stated as follows: "The key trait of a vital, dynamic corporation is looking reality (the truth) straight in the eye, and then acting upon it with as much speed as possible."

Welch clearly realized that facing the truth can be very difficult and often uncomfortable. It's challenging to get people to see a situation for what it really is and not what they hope it will be. Our emotions can lead us away from the truth, and often cause us to be gripped by self-delusion and other false perceptions of reality.

There is a great deal of applicability in Welch's observation, but particularly as it relates to the problems we face in life. If we are in fact on a quest for truth and wisdom, we will face our problems as quickly as we can. Unfortunately, most of us don't do this because we are, perhaps unknowingly, on a quest for pleasure and happiness. Having to grapple with painful problems is in conflict with the pursuit of pleasant feelings. As a result, we ignore the difficult problems facing us, leaving them alone in hopes they will simply go away.

* * *

Finally, our great pursuit of pleasure and happiness explains why we struggle to establish good habits yet at the same time have difficulty breaking our bad habits.

Dr. Tom Morris shares some helpful insights into this quandary. Good habits usually result from thoughtful, rational decision making plus personal discipline and repetition. When establishing a new habit, getting started is generally the hardest part. For example, we might start a new exercise and diet routine because we observe our bodies slowly deteriorating or we know of people our age who've suffered heart attacks. We calculate a shortfall in our retirement needs and tighten our budgets so we can direct more financial resources to our retirement accounts. As we implement these necessary changes over time, they become permanent habits in our lives, and ultimately will lead to our future well-being.

Bad habits, on the other hand, are usually not the result

of logical thought or careful deliberation. Frequently, they are a result of pleasurable sensations that make us feel good. And if it results in making us feel better, then we are prone to doing it again and again. Repetition sets in and behold—a new habit has formed.

In this day and time, good feelings often have far greater power over our ability to reason. Once established, these bad habits are much more difficult to break because they are rooted in the strength of personal feelings and pleasurable sensations. It's essential to always be careful to avoid bad habits whenever possible. In the following chapters, we will explore how to overcome bad habits and replace them with good ones.

It is vital that each of us is honest and asks him- or herself: Am I on a truth and wisdom quest or on a pleasure and feel-good quest? These two pursuits will almost always lead us in opposite directions.

Seeking the Easy Path

A third reason people avoid the path leading to excellence is because they are often looking for shortcuts. C. S. Lewis addressed this issue when he said that the ancients always recognized wisdom as the answer to life's chief problems. People should therefore first seek to understand the principles that govern life, and then live in harmony with them. Lewis is suggesting that the problem with modern people is they are always looking for ways to make life work in accordance with what they want.

Stated differently, and as it pertains to our topic, many would say, "I want a life of excellence, but I don't want to go down the long, difficult path to get it." So, we seek shortcuts. We think this can be accomplished through easy formulas and techniques. Examples can be seen in the self-help section of any large bookstore. One will encounter such books as *5 Simple Steps to Double Your Sales,* or *7 Easy Ways to Make Big Money in the Stock Market.* In today's world, if you have a problem, it is very likely someone has a ready formula or technique that claims to help you easily overcome it.

I often see this in counseling people who have pain in their lives. They desire immediate relief. Recently, a man who had been married for a number of years came to see me because his marriage had unraveled. As he told me his story, it was evident that the marriage was in shambles as a result of the path he and his wife had been on for so many years. The man was a typical Type A personality. He wanted to get things done quickly, and was hoping a forty-five-minute counseling session would solve his marital problems. He hoped I might have some type of formula that would untangle the mess they had made of their marriage. I reminded him that it had taken years to get to this low point in his life and there was no quick fix. I then posed the question "Are you willing to get on a different path, one that may be long and difficult but that will eventually lead to healing, forgiveness, and restoration of your marriage?" He said he was willing.

Dr. Rick Jensen is a nationally recognized sports psychologist whose clients include more than fifty touring pros on the PGA, LPGA, and Champions Tours. Fourteen of his clients have won at least one major championship. He has said that even professional golfers are so often looking for some kind of quick swing fix or putting cure. Jensen comments:

> *Golfers don't want to hear that the reason they're not getting any better is because they don't practice, or that their expectations for what it takes to learn and to play good golf are flawed. What they want is to see their swings on video and then saved to a DVD, so they can show their pals what it is they're working on; or, they want a quick fix that will cure that slice with minimal effort. Instead, what generally happens is the tip they*

get doesn't transfer to the course under pressure, and they wind up blaming their teacher and walking across the street to see another pro. Or they go and buy a book or read a magazine article in hopes of finding a better tip that is the magic pill they're seeking.

Maybe this is why a leading literary critic believes the Harry Potter series sold millions of copies. It is full of wish-fulfillment fantasies. The lead character could simply wave a magic wand and instantly make things happen. The critic said, "This is one of the primary fantasies of the human heart." Magic is so much more appealing than painful disciplined effort.

In reality, there is an art to living, and in order to make progress on life's meaningful objectives, steady plodding along the right path is required. Steady, patient, and often unexciting steps are the most effective way to make substantial progress in life. This doesn't have much appeal to people caught up in our instant-gratification culture. Excellence is not a door one can easily walk through and find instant results. A life of excellence is a long, patient quest that does not come quickly.

English minister William Carey is a great example of a successful plodder. Despite little formal education, by his teenage years he could read six different languages. Because of his linguistic skills, he was chosen for an important missionary position in India, and later became professor of Oriental languages at Fort William College in Calcutta. He also founded his own publishing company, which printed Bibles in forty different languages and dialects, and were distributed to more than 300 million people.

When Carey was asked how he was able to accomplish so much, he replied that he was a good plodder. In his own words: "Anything beyond this will be too much. I can plod. That is my only genius. I can persevere in any definite pursuit. To this I owe everything."

In summary, there is an art to living, and it is not a quick, easy formula. The final outcome of our lives is determined by the paths we go down, and every path has a predictable ultimate destination.

Chapter 4
Changing Your Life

We are what we repeatedly do.
Excellence is not an art but a habit.
— Aristotle

So where do we go from here? How do we change the direction of our lives? How do we move from the life we are presently living to the life we really want?

To be blunt, it starts when we stop deluding ourselves and choose to embrace the truth and acknowledge that we may not be on the right path.

C.S. Lewis said,

When you come to a fork in the road and find you have taken the wrong road, don't keep pressing forward trying to prove you were right. You promptly turn back to the fork in the road and embark on the right road.

Similar to Lewis's thinking, Scott Peck wrote in his best-selling book *The Road Less Traveled*,

> *The more clearly we see the reality of the world, the better equipped we are to deal with the world. The less clearly we see the reality of the world—the more our minds are befuddled by falsehood, misperceptions, and illusions—the less able we will be to determine correct courses of action and make wise decisions. Our view of reality is like a map with which to negotiate the terrain of life. If the map is true and accurate, we will generally know where we are, and if we have decided where we want to go, we will generally know how to get there. If the map is false and inaccurate, we generally will be lost, stumbling in the darkness.*

Understanding Yourself

It is essential to know who you really are. Philosopher Dallas Willard notes, if you are going to take care of something, you have to understand it, be it a rosebush, a tomato plant, or a car engine. If we really want to care for our lives we must understand ourselves.

Peter Drucker, one of the world's foremost business

consultants, believed it was crucial to understand our strengths and weaknesses in order to determine our unique roles in life. He said, "When you know who you are, you will be comfortable in making decisions about your future."

I would add that a good starting place is to seek to understand your personal flaws. As radio personality Hugh Hewitt relates

> *George W. Bush drank too much. He stopped. He would not have been president had he not stopped. It's that simple. ... A high-ranking academic stored pornography on his computer. The porn was discovered when he asked the university to expand the storage [capacity] of his machine. He was obliged to resign. His flaws crushed his career.*

Regardless of who you are, we all have flaws. We are all dysfunctional in some way or other, but the people who achieve excellence in life ruthlessly study themselves and bring their flaws under control.

I think about it in terms of the game of golf. Whenever my game goes in the tank, I know there's a flaw somewhere in my grip, my posture, or my swing. When

I take a lesson, the golf pro videos my swing, and can then explain to me what I'm doing wrong. Not until I can truly see what my problem is can I begin the process of correcting it.

Isn't it remarkable what we will do for our golf game but will rarely consider for our lives?

The Vector Principle

A second crucial idea comes from author John Maxwell, who wisely stated, "You will never change your life until you change something you do daily."

In order to grasp the significance of these very simple, yet very profound words, let us consider the second important principle. It's called the Vector Principle, and I was introduced to it in Jerry Foster's book, *Life Focus*. Foster describes the Vector Principle in these terms:

> *Vector, a term in mathematics and physics, quantifies the speed and direction of an object. If you were the pilot of a jetliner, you would use vectors to define the course to your destination. When you are given a new vector by the control center, you turn the plane to line up with that heading on the compass, creating a new vector angle. Obviously, even the smallest vector*

change in the cockpit can make a big difference in the plane's ultimate destination. Though it may seem an imperceptible change, with every mile traveled you are farther from your previous course. For example, you could make a tiny vector change while flying between New York and Seattle and end up in Los Angeles instead. Some vectors require a drastic change of direction, such as taking off the west and vectoring 180 degrees for an eastbound flight. However, most flights are achieved through a series of rather small vectors, minor turns and course adjustments that allow the cockpit crew to fly the plane from point A to point B.

The Vector Principle applies to our lives in the same manner. Even if you never fly an airplane, you are vectoring through life by the choices you make. You are currently on a course that was determined by choices you have made since you were aware of your capacity to choose. Many of these choices seemed rather insignificant at the time, but small changes make a big difference over time.

Those final words, "small changes make a big difference over time," are very significant. We so often believe that radical corrections are needed in order to experience meaningful change in our lives; however, most of us have a difficult time sustaining large-scale changes, and often give up. Take New Years' resolutions, for example. We make these grand plans for personal improvement, yet very often they aren't reasonable. While we have great intentions for our lives, they don't get us on a path to excellence.

Nido Quebin, a prominent businessman and college president, has made this observation:

One of the greatest reasons people cannot mobilize themselves, is that they are always dreaming of some grand accomplishment that they hope one day will come to pass. Most worthwhile achievements are the result of many little things done in a single [strategic] direction.

In Donald Phillips' book *Lincoln on Leadership*, Phillips shows how Abraham Lincoln used this approach in his strategy to win the Civil War:

Lincoln realized that the attainment of such a successful outcome had to be accomplished in small steps. So he constantly set specific short-term goals that his generals and cabinet members could focus on with intent and immediacy. Early in the war, he established such strategic objectives as blockading key Southern ports, gaining control of the Mississippi River, and rebuilding and training the military. Throughout the war, he concentrated on defeating Lee's army as opposed to the capture of the Confederate capital. And he took one battle at a time rather than trying to win them all at once.

Being Productive

I try to make small, incremental changes each year so they become new habits that slowly and surely lead to personal transformation. These changes will make a radical difference if they remain with me over the course of my life. It generally takes time, however, to see any noticeable results.

As I look back over my own life, the most significant change I made was when I was twenty-four years old. After reading a biography on the life of John Wesley, I realized that in order for me to use my time wisely, I would need to wake up much earlier each day during the workweek. It was extremely difficult at first, but now, thirty-five years later, it's routine for me to get up at 5:15 AM. This simple discipline has enabled me to create more time for purposeful use. I use these early morning hours to deepen my relationship with God, enjoy physical exercise, and read *The Wall Street Journal*. As a result, I'm able to accomplish a great deal before my actual workday has even begun.

At the first of every year, I now seek to make several small changes that will become permanent in my life. I've found that if I focus on just a few small changes, they create momentum, which in turn impacts other areas of my life. You could almost say there's a ripple effect.

In his best-selling book *The Power of Habit,* Charles Duhigg shares a story that illustrates the power of the rippling effect.

Back in 1987, Alcoa hired Paul O'Neil as its new CEO. Alcoa, which had been in business for over 100 years, was struggling and needed new leadership. O'Neil was a former government bureaucrat that no one had ever heard of.

The company scheduled an investor meeting in a large New York ballroom to introduce O'Neil for the first time. The room was packed as he began his remarks.

I want to talk to you about worker safety. Every year, numerous Alcoa workers are injured so badly that they miss a day of work. Our safety record is better than the general American workforce, especially considering that our employees work with metals that are 1,500 degrees and machines that can rip a man's arm off. But it's not good enough. I intend to make Alcoa the safest company in America. I intend to go for zero injuries.

O'Neil hadn't said anything about profits. He didn't mention taxes. There was no talk of "using alignment to achieve a win-win synergistic market advantage." For all anyone in the audience knew, given his talk of worker safety, O'Neill might be pro-regulation, or worse, a Democrat. It was a terrifying prospect.

Eventually, someone raised a hand and asked about inventories in the aerospace division. Another asked about the company's capital ratios. O'Neill said:

I'm not certain you heard me. If you want to understand how Alcoa is doing, you need to look at our workplace safety figures. If we bring our injury rates down, it won't be because of cheerleading or the nonsense you sometimes hear from other CEOs. It will be because the individuals at this company have agreed to become part of something important: They've devoted themselves to creating a habit of excellence. Safety will be an indicator that we're making progress in changing our habits across the entire institution. That's how we should be judged.

The investors in the room almost stampeded out the doors when the presentation ended. One jogged to the lobby, found a pay phone, and called his twenty largest clients.

"I said, 'The board put a crazy hippie in charge and he's going to kill the company,'" that investor told me. "'I ordered them to sell their stock immediately, before everyone else in the room started calling their clients and telling them the same thing. "It was literally the worst piece of advice I gave in my entire career.'"

Within a year of O'Neill's speech, Alcoa's profits hit a record high. By the time O'Neill retired in 2000, the company's annual net income was five times larger than before he arrived, and its market capitalization had risen by $27 billion. Someone who invested $1 million in Alcoa on the day O'Neill was hired would have earned another million in dividends while he headed the company, and the value of their stock would have been five times greater when he left.

What's more, all the growth occurred while Alcoa became one of the safest companies in the world. Before O'Neill's arrival, almost every Alcoa plant had at least one accident per week. Once his safety plan was implemented, some facilities would go years without a single employee losing a workday due to an accident. The company's worker injury rate fell to one-twentieth of the US average.

So how did O'Neill make one of the largest, stodgiest, and most potentially dangerous companies into a profit machine and a bastion of safety? By attacking one habit and then watching the changes ripple through the organization.

"I knew I had to transform Alcoa," O'Neill told me. "But you can't order people to change. That's not how the brain works. So I decided I was going to start by focusing on one thing. If I could start disrupting the habits around one thing, it would spread throughout the entire company."

Your Personal Challenge

Take the time to look at the most important areas of your life. Choose one or two incremental changes you know will make a positive impact, and put them into practice till they become a permanent part of your life. Eventually these changes will become permanent habits that are almost second nature, and you will then want to seek additional changes as you gain momentum. You'll begin to see the Vector Principle at work, and understand that small changes really do make a significant difference over time. What most people don't realize is that the big payoff comes from the compounding effect over years of repetition. Small changes that are strategically directed toward important goals can lead to great accomplishments and ultimately to the treasured prize of a life of excellence.

Note: At the end of this book is a list of some basic ideas for change you might want to consider.

Chapter 5
Time is of the Essence

The earlier you start making small changes,
the more powerfully the effect of compounding
works in your favor.
—Darren Hardy

After reading Andy Stanley's book *The Best Question Ever,* I was left with a strong conviction that a life of excellence depends on how wisely we invest our time. As he points out, "There is a cumulative value to investing small amounts of time in certain activities over a long period of time." I would emphasize the combination of two words: "cumulative value."

Cumulative value has application to every area of a person's life. For example, we know there's clearly a cumulative effect if you exercise thirty-five to forty minutes a day, five days a week, over a forty-year period. This consistent, disciplined activity is in stark contrast to a sedentary life over that same period of time. It's important to note, however, that the value of physical exercise is not found in any one particular day. Exercise has a compounding effect; it's the consistent, incremental investment of time that makes a lasting difference.

This is also true if you're investing in relationships, your spiritual life, or in your finances. It was Albert Einstein who said, "Compound interest is the most powerful force in the universe."

Darren Hard, in his book *The Compound Effect,* shares the illustration of the magic penny. If you were given the choice of receiving $3 million in cash right now or a single penny that would double in value every day for thirty-one days, which would you choose? Most people impulsively choose the $3 million in cash. But if you chose the penny, on day five you would have sixteen cents, and on day ten $5.12. After twenty days, with only eleven left, you would have $5,243. This is when the power of compounding begins its rapid ascent. On day thirty-one you would have $10,737,418.24.

Pennies seem so insignificant, even when they're doubling in value in the first few days. It's only with the passage of time that a paltry penny becomes a vast amount of money. Hardy says that very few things are as impressive as the magic of compounding pennies, and what we don't realize is that this same compounding force is equally powerful in every area of our lives.

The cumulative effect of investing small amounts of time in certain carefully chosen activities over a long period of time can best be understood in the third and final principle. It is called The Daffodil Principle, written by Jaroldeen Edwards.

Several times my daughter had telephoned to say, "Mother, you must come see the daffodils before they are over." I wanted to go, but it was a two-hour drive from Laguna to Lake Arrowhead. "I will come next Tuesday," I promised, a little reluctantly, on her third call.

Next Tuesday dawned cold and rainy. Still, I had promised, and so I drove there. When I finally walked into Carolyn's house and hugged and greeted my grandchildren, I said, "Forget the daffodils, Carolyn! The road is invisible in the clouds and fog, and there is nothing in the world except you and these children that I want to see bad enough to drive another inch!"

My daughter smiled calmly and said, "We drive in this all the time, Mother."

"Well, you won't get me back on the road until it clears, and then I'm heading for home!" I assured her.

"I was hoping you'd take me over to the garage to pick up my car."

"How far will we have to drive?"

"Just a few blocks," Carolyn said. "I'll drive. I'm used to this."

After several minutes, I had to ask, "Where are we going? This isn't the way to the garage!"

"We're going to my garage the long way," Carolyn smiled, "by way of the daffodils."

"Carolyn," I said sternly, "please turn around."

"It's all right, Mother, I promise. You will never forgive yourself if you miss this experience."

After about twenty minutes, we turned onto a small gravel road and I saw a small church. On the far side of the church, I saw a hand-lettered sign with an arrow that read, DAFFODIL GARDEN. We got out of the car and each took a child's hand, and I followed Carolyn down the path. Then, we turned a corner of the path, and I looked up and gasped. Before me lay the most glorious sight.

It looked as though someone had taken a great vat of gold and poured it over the mountain peak *and its surrounding slopes. The flowers were planted in majestic, swirling patterns—great ribbons and swaths of deep orange, white, lemon yellow, salmon pink, saffron, and butter yellow. Each different-colored variety was planted as a group so that it swirled and flowed like its own river with its own unique hue. There were five acres of flowers.*

"But who has done it?" I asked Carolyn.

"It's just one woman," Carolyn answered. "She lives on the property. That's her home." Carolyn pointed to a well-kept A-frame house that looked small and modest in the midst of all that glory. We walked up to the house. On the patio, we saw a poster. Answers to the Questions I Know You Are Asking was the headline.

The first answer was a simple one: 50,000 bulbs, it read. The second answer was "One at a time, by one woman. Two hands, two feet, very little brain." The third answer was "Began in 1958."

There it was, The Daffodil Principle. For me, that moment was a life-changing experience. I thought of this woman whom I had never met, who, more than forty years before, had begun - one bulb at a time - to bring her vision of beauty and joy to an obscure mountaintop. Still, just planting one bulb at a time, year after year, had changed the world. This unknown woman had forever changed the world in which she lived. She had created something indescribable: magnificence, beauty, and inspiration.

The principle her daffodil garden taught is one of the greatest principles of celebration. That is, learning to move toward our goals and desires one step at a time—often just one baby-step at time—and learning to love the doing, learning to use the accumulation of time. When we multiply tiny pieces of time with small increments of daily effort, we too will find we can accomplish magnificent things. We can change the world.

"It makes me sad in a way," I admitted to Carolyn. "What might I have accomplished if I had thought of a wonderful goal thirty-five or forty years ago and had worked away at it 'one bulb at a time' through all those years? Just think what I might have been able to achieve!"

My daughter summed up the message of the day in her usual direct way. "Start tomorrow," she said.

It's so pointless to think of the lost hours of yesterdays. The way to make learning a lesson of celebration instead of a cause for regret is to only ask, "How can I put this to use today?"

How do you change the course of your life? How do you begin to achieve a life of excellence? Learn to use the accumulation of time. Multiply tiny pieces of time with small increments of daily effort and you can accomplish magnificent things—you can achieve a life of excellence.

But you must put this to use today.

Concluding Thought

If we do not seize and take hold of our limited time, then our days will continually be devoured by random, unproductive activities that ultimately add up to a lot of wasted time. Novelist Robert Heinlein said, "In the absence of clearly defined goals, we become strangely loyal to performing daily trivia until we become enslaved by it."

Because our time is, in fact, our very life, if we waste our time, we will waste our lives. Further, it is essential to grasp, that if we do not invest regular amounts of time into the important activities of life, the effects of compounding can work in reverse. Neglect is like an ever-growing snowball that has a cumulative negative effect. It can lead to a vicious downward spiral that can bring a great deal of pain and disappointment into our lives.

Finally (and it would be impossible to overstate its importance), in the most important areas of your life, you cannot make up for lost time. Never. I remember back in college, friends would goof off during the semester and then, at exam time, pull all-nighters and cram in hope of making up for their neglect. Some were able to pull it off; most were not. This strategy does not work in real life. When it comes to relationships, for instance, you can't cram or pull an all-nighter. I've seen this happen in many marriages. Over the years, some men become less and less attentive to their wives until one day they are stunned when they're served with divorce papers. It is often only then that they're motivated to change their ways; yet it's too late, for their wives have decided to move on.

This is equally true in the world of investing. Financially, you can't wait till you're sixty to start saving for retirement.

The most important areas of your life require regular deposits of time as the years go by. If you miss these opportunities, they are lost forever.

* * *

I am very much like Carolyn's mother in the story of the daffodils. Being fifty-nine years old, I often wish I had understood these principles back when I was twenty-one. Of course there's nothing I can do about the past, but I'm challenged by those final words in her story. It's pointless to think of the lost hours of yesterday. The way to make learning a lesson of celebration instead of a cause of regret is to only ask, "How can I put this to use today?"

While we can't change the past, we are responsible for what we do with the rest of our lives. I continually challenge the men I work with to sprint across the finish line. It doesn't matter how old you are or where you are in your life's journey; the ideas in this book need to be recognized and integrated into your life. Remember, this is your life, so take a look at the path you are now traveling, and seek to determine what vector turns you need to make.

If you want to have an exceptional life, a life of excellence, and truly reach the potential God has endowed you with, you must walk certain paths that most people are not willing to walk. But when you do, it will make all the difference in the quality of your life and the legacy you leave behind.

To conclude, I leave you with the same challenge Mr. Keating presented to his students:

"Since your final destiny has yet to be determined, why not make it extraordinary and leave a lasting legacy?"

An Action Plan

This section is intended to provide you some final thoughts and ideas that I hope will stimulate your creative juices and help you ignite action.

1. Let Life Flourish

Aristotle, who lived 350 years before Christ, was probably the first person to develop a simple plan for personal transformation. He believed it all begins by developing a goal, what he called the *telos*.

This should be the ultimate aim of your life. Then you must specifically outline the steps that will enable you to reach these goals. This is a process of training by which you form habits that eventually become second nature to you.

Finally this would lead to what Aristotle described as *eudaimonia*, which some would interpret as meaning happiness. In reality, however, Aristotle meant "a life that flourishes."

2. Change Daily

Remember the wise words of John Maxwell: "You will never change your life until you change something you do daily." These changes need to be directed toward the most important objectives in your life.

3. Invest in Yourself

We need to recognize that the efforts to make these changes are actually an investment in ourselves. Stephen Covey has said that we are "instruments of our own performance." If we are going to live effectively, it is essential that we devote time to our personal development.

4. Fifteen Minutes

Unless you're already an early riser, I urge you to consider waking up earlier during the five-day workweek. I suggest you start by getting up fifteen minutes earlier. At the end of six weeks, move the alarm clock back another fifteen minutes. Continue this till you reach a reasonable wakeup hour that you can sustain. I am reminded that Thomas Jefferson, Benjamin Franklin, and George Washington Carver all attributed rising early as a key factor in leading a productive life. Franklin was serious when he said, "Early to bed, early to rise, makes a man healthy, wealthy, and wise." Remember, you are creating additional time for productive use.

5. Trade Bad for Good

Seek to replace a bad habit with a good one. For instance, if television absorbs too much of your time, then I suggest selecting a good book and going down to a local coffee shop or some other suitable location to read for an hour or two each evening. I recommend you read books that will impact your spiritual life, your marriage and family, and your career. Frequently I have more than one book going at any given time. You will find that eventually reading a book is far more enjoyable — and beneficial — than watching TV.

6. Work the Memory

The research is clear: if you don't use your mind, it will lose clarity and sharpness as the years go by. One of the best ways to exercise your mind is through memory work. Consider memorizing important quotations, Bible verses, new vocabulary words, or important information that relates to your work. In fact, if you have a college education and learn three new vocabulary words each week (which takes about ten minutes a day), in five to seven years you will master the English language.

7. Selective Multitasking

Consider performing two tasks at the same time. Take a long walk and do memory work, or listen to an informative recorded message on your iPod. Ride a stationary bike and read a book at the same time. I like to walk and pray.

8. Use the Right Tools

Technology has enabled us to listen to a variety of high-quality presentations and messages that increase our knowledge. These can easily be downloaded and listened to while exercising, driving, flying, or using mass transportation. Our website, www.thecenterbham.org, features over seventy recorded messages. Other excellent learning websites include: www.ted.com and www.coursera.org.

9. Think Big, Start Small

Very often we face large tasks that we need to tackle but that appear so overwhelming that we have a hard time getting started. I suggest you begin by working on the task thirty to forty minutes a day. Once you begin to see progress, you'll be motivated to complete the task much sooner than you initially expected.

10. Compounding Interest

Remember that the earlier you start implementing small changes in your life, the more powerfully the magic of compounding works to your advantage. A terrific example of this is to consider a person in his or her twenties who each year invests the maximum amount that can be deposited into a tax0-deferred IRA. If this is done annually over a forty-year period, he or she can expect to reap a huge financial windfall.

11. Pressing Importance

Stephen Covey has observed that the healthiest, most productive people are those who have the discipline to focus time and energy on the important but not urgent activities of life. These can include planning, continuing education, reading, developing new personal relationships, investing in your spiritual life, and physical exercise. Please note that none of these activities is especially pressing, but they are essential if you intend to continue to grow and develop.

12. The Clock and the Compass

Finally, Covey reminds us that our great struggle to live effectively can be best understood by contrasting two of the most powerful tools in our lives: the clock and the compass. The clock represents how we manage our time. This includes our schedules, appointments, activities, and what we do with our free time. The compass, on the other hand, represents what is important to us: Our values, our goals, and our mission in life. Inevitably, we struggle because the clock is not in harmony with the compass in our lives, and therefore what we do with our time does not in any way contribute to what's most important to us and to what we're trying to accomplish.

* * *

The message in this book originated when I was asked to address the management team of a large corporation. My sole objective was to give these business leaders some guiding principles on how to live more wisely and effectively both in their careers and personal lives.

Since that time I have had the privilege of sharing these ideas at a number of corporate events and private business conferences, as well as with athletic teams and even with the graduating class of a boys' prep school.

Regardless of a person's age, this message always seems to resonate. I believe this is because we all share the same challenge: We intend to live a certain type of life, but avoid the necessary and difficult measures required to see this become a reality.

As a Christian speaker and author, I'm often asked what role God should play in bringing about transformation in our lives. This is an appropriate question, particularly as it pertains to the transformation of the heart. Too many people assume that being a Christian is about trying to live a good moral life on their own power. In reality, the historic Christian faith as made clear in the Bible is all about the life of God working in the hearts and souls of men and women. God seeks to transform hearts, to lead and guide and to dispense wisdom and understanding to His people.

This is, however, not a book about spiritual transformation. If you are interested in that subject, I highly recommend one of my previous books, *The True Measure of a Man* (jimbo@truemeasureofaman.com).

This is a practical book about how to structure your life and equip yourself to be more disciplined so that you're prepared to live out your purpose in life. It seeks to help you discover the true path that leads to a life of excellence.

* * *

I wish I had understood these principles much earlier. What a difference it would have made in my life. However, I will be forever grateful that just five years ago, at the age of fifty-four I developed a clear understanding of these truths. Without question, these principles have made a significant difference in my life. So many of the small changes which I have made are now habits, and have positively impacted my relationship with God, my marriage, the parenting of my children, my physical well being, and my own personal knowledge. Depending on how many years I have left to live, I look forward to seeing the ripple effect of compounding as the years go by. My prayer is that these same principles will have an equally dramatic effect on your life, and that when you come to the end of your days, you will be able to rest in the knowledge of having achieved a life of excellence.

Sources

Covey, Sean. *The 7 Habits of Highly Effective Teens.* New York: Simon & Schuster, 1998.

Covey, Stephen. *The 7 Habits of Highly Effective People.* New York: Simon & Schuster, 1989. With A. Roger Merrill and Rebecca R. Merrill. *First Things First.* New York: Simon & Schuster, 1994.

Duhigg, Charles. *The Power of Habit.* New York: Random House Publishing, 2012.

Fisher, Bob and Judy Fisher. *Life Is A Gift: Inspiration From The Soon Departed.* New York: Faith Words, Hachette Book Group, 2008.

Foster, Jerry. *Life Focus: Achieving a Life of Purpose & Influence.* Grand Rapids: Revell Publishing, 2004.

Hardy, Darren. *The Compound Effect.* New York: Vanguard Press, Perseus Books Group, 2010.

Hewitt, Hugh. *In, But Not Of: A Guide to Christian Ambition.* Nashville: Thomas Nelson, Inc., 2010.

Jeffress, Robert Dr. *The Solomon Secrets.* Colorado Springs: WaterBrook Press, 2002.

Jensen, Rick Dr. and Dave Allen. *Easier Said Than Done.* Seattle: Sea Script Company, 2010.

Maxwell, John C. *The 15 Invaluable Laws of Growth.* New York: Center Street, Hachette Book Group, 2012.

Maxwell, John C. *Today Matters: 12 Daily Practices To Guarantee Tomorrow's Success.* New York: Warner Faith, Time Warner Book Group, 2004.

MacDonald, Gordon. *Ordering Your Private World.* Nashville, Thomas Nelson Publishers, 1985.

Morris, Tom. *The Art of Achievement: Mastering the 7 C's of Success in Business and Life.* Kansas City: Andrews McMeel Publishing, 2002.

Morris, Tom, PhD. *True Success: A New Philosophy of Excellence.* New York: Berkley, 1994.

Peck, M. Scott. *The Road Less Traveled.* New York: Simon & Schuster, 1978.

Stanley, Andy. *The Best Question Ever: A Revolutionary Approach to Decision Making.* Colorado Springs: Multnomah Books, 2004.

Stanley, Andy. *The Principle of the Path.* Nashville: Thomas Nelson, Inc. 2008.

Willard, Dallas. *The Spirit of the Disciplines: Understanding How God Changes Lives.* New York: HarperCollins Publishers, 1991.

Wooden, Coach John and stave Jamison. *The Wisdom of Wooden: My Century On and Off the Court.* New York: McGraw Hill, 2010.

Wright, Nicholas Thomas. *After You Believe: Why Christian Character Matters.* New York: HarperCollins Publishers, 2010.

About the Author

Richard E. Simmons III received his BA from the University of the South (Sewanee) in Economics in 1976. He later studied Risk Management and Insurance at Georgia State University prior to beginning a twenty-five-year career with Hilb, Rogal, and Hamilton, a property and casualty insurance firm where he was CEO for ten years. Simmons has devoted much of his life to giving back to the community by advising businessmen and professionals. Through these experiences, he discovered he had a calling for teaching and public speaking. In December 2000 Simmons founded the Center for Executive Leadership, a not-for-profit, faith-based ministry. When he's not with his wife and three children, you'll find him teaching, counseling, writing, or speaking to men's groups across the country.

Also by the Author

SAFE PASSAGE

This book examines C.S Lewis's thoughts and perspective on the issue of human mortality.

www.thecenterbham.org

Also by the Author

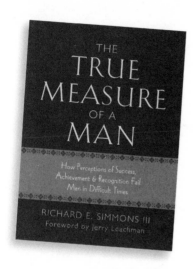

THE TRUE
MEASURE
OF A MAN

*In our performance driven culture,
this book provides liberating truth on
how to be set free from the fear of failure,
comparing ourselves to others, and the
false ideas we have about masculinity.*

www.thecenterbham.org

Also by the Author

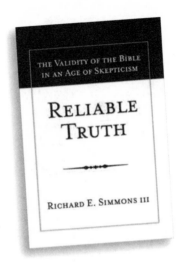

RELIABLE
TRUTH

*This book offers powerful and
compelling evidence why the Bible is valid
and true.*

www.thecenterbham.org

Also by the Author

WISDOM
Life's Great
Treasure

"My hope is that this book serves as a guide to help you walk in wisdom on your joourney toward a healthy and meaningful life." –Richard E. Simmons

www.thecenterbham.org

Also by the Author

SEX
AT FIRST
SIGHT

This book explains the hookup culture - how it came about, how it is affecting our younger generation and finally, God's intent for our sexuality.

www.thecenterbham.org

Author Contact Information

*Richard E. Simmons III welcomes inquiries
and is available for speaking opportunities.*

For information on scheduling,
contact:

JIMBO HEAD AT
jimbo@TheCenterBham.org

Visit our website at:
www.TheCenterBham.org

UNION HILL
PUBLISHING